CW00840172

Tim Wigham grew up in Southern Africa and has dual British and South African citizenship; he served in the British Commandos for eight years between 1992 and 2000 before completing his full-time MBA in Cape Town, 2001.

Tim then specialised in the facilitation of SME executive leadership breakaways across a range of industries to build strong cohesion, as well as clear strategy, mission, vision, and authentic company values.

In the sports industry, Tim worked on mental toughness with several of the Springbok Rugby players who went on to be World Cup winners in 2007.

Tim has worked as a performance improvement expert in the offshore-oil-and-gas industry since 2008 and now advises project leaders on team performance solutions in the global energy sector.

Tim is based in the North East of Scotland; he is married and has three young children. His main interests include writing, reading, travel, and CrossFit. He also enjoys blogging about inspiration.

!NSPIRED

PERFORMANCE COACHING INSIGHTS FROM THE FRONT LINE

TIM WIGHAM

authorHOUSE®

AuthorHouse™ UK
1663 Liberty Drive
Bloomington, IN 47403 USA
www.authorhouse.co.uk
Phone: 0800.197.4150

© 2017 Tim Wigham. All rights reserved.

No part of this book may be reproduced, stored in a retrieval system, or transmitted by any means without the written permission of the author.

Published by AuthorHouse 04/19/2017

ISBN: 978-1-5246-6827-3 (sc)
ISBN: 978-1-5246-6826-6 (e)

Print information available on the last page.

Any people depicted in stock imagery provided by Thinkstock are models, and such images are being used for illustrative purposes only. Certain stock imagery © Thinkstock.

This book is printed on acid-free paper.

Because of the dynamic nature of the Internet, any web addresses or links contained in this book may have changed since publication and may no longer be valid. The views expressed in this work are solely those of the author and do not necessarily reflect the views of the publisher, and the publisher hereby disclaims any responsibility for them.

CONTENTS

For my father,
Jonathan Wigham,
the brightest mind I ever knew

You inspired my interest in becoming
an author and departed this world with too many
unpublished books of your own.

CHAPTER 1

ARE YOU READY FOR THE NEXT CHALLENGE?

Here are three important considerations as we prepare for the year ahead and the challenges it will hold:

1. Do we have the right people involved? A successful campaign in 2015 reinforced for me the importance of the right team mindset from the outset. This is driven by respected leaders and committed team members.
2. Do we have the right disciplines in place? Time is a precious commodity in today's project environment, so ensuring that we use it wisely, and that we focus on the disciplines that give us the best return for our collective investment, is essential.

3. Do we understand the purpose of our work? I have noticed that success is much more likely when objectives are clearly defined and communicated on a regular basis. The purpose unites the people and inspires the process.

Whatever the next year throws at you, a united team with smart disciplines and clarity of purpose will be in a strong position to succeed!

Have a great year.

CHAPTER 2

HOW DO YOU REDUCE THE OPERATIONAL COST?

With cost reduction at the forefront of everyone's mind at the moment, it may seem strange to consider an "optional" service provider of performance-improvement coaching, but operational cost reduction through enhanced process efficiency and accelerated team learning, whilst safely achieving all well objectives, is exactly what Exceed has been associated with since 2005.

Investing in a proven, impartial, external resource to provide appropriate support pre-execution, and to drive the right people/process disciplines on the rig during the execution phase, has helped teams realise a significant investment return on both short campaigns, where it is essential to get it right the first time, and on longer campaigns, where continuous improvement and consistency (versus complacency) are imperative.

In our client's experience, a focus on always bringing the right people together, and an emphasis on always rigorously planning and reviewing their business, has always enabled the team involved to safely achieve objectives within the planned budget overall. The project savings from this high-performance approach always significantly outweigh the optional investment in the right performance-improvement coaching resource.

Cost reduction is a by-product of an exceptional team working exceptionally well together. With the right people and the right approach, the right results will follow.

Have a safe and cost-efficient year.

CHAPTER 3

HOW DO YOU EVIDENCE THE VALUE OF PERFORMANCE-COACHING SUPPORT?

It is essential that customers of a performance-coaching service have clarity and transparency when evidencing the return on the investment made in that external resource.

Recent projects have shown us that the right focus prior to execution can ensure fewer mistakes are made early on thanks to risk mitigation, the application of transferable learning through shared experience, and rigorous challenge to the plan. On a drilling campaign, this means that the first well will likely be drilled more safely and more efficiently (cost effectively) than it would be if a less rigorous approach is taken during the pre-execution phase.

Applying this necessary rigour takes significant time and effort. In theory, it can be done by someone within the operator team. In reality, those individuals are already at capacity completing their own daily tasks and troubleshooting daily issues as execution mobilisation looms ever closer. A performance coach with relevant experience and bespoke tools, who is accountable for harnessing the collective expertise of the project team and for ensuring risks and actions are closed in a timely manner, will significantly increase the chances of the project team getting the first well right, first time.

Evidencing the value of this rigorous approach can be done by calculating the time (and cost) saved through harnessed changes (captured and embedded lessons/suggestions) to the original plan, whether in the form of smarter technology, more efficient processes, or additional expertise. On our last project, upfront savings pre-execution already more than paid for the coaching overhead for the entire project.

During project execution, leadership and team commitment and an uncompromising approach to the disciplines of advance planning and after-action review, as well as a regular lessons-learned conference call, undeniably accelerate the natural learning curve. This also enables a strong safety culture through communication, awareness, and teamwork.

Again, an ever-present, versatile coach who is embedded within the execution team and is accountable for capturing, tracking, and closing any and all opportunities on behalf of the team will drive a quantifiable improvement in efficiency (and cost reduction). This improvement would be slower without this resource whose sole remit and focus is the implementation and utilisation of proven disciplines and tools and who is not distracted by real-time operations management.

It is especially during the first several wells of a drilling campaign that the "perfect storm" occurs; the team is still settling into a familiar rhythm, problems are encountered for the first time, and lesson after lesson comes rolling in. It is at this stage that a qualified, driven, and experienced performance-coaching resource delivers the multiple return on the initial investment. The reason for this is that the early lessons that are captured, tracked, and closed, and that apply to every subsequent well (often several times a well), will clearly save the most time (and cost) overall.

Not to belabour the point, but without a dedicated resource who is focused on this responsibility, it is very unlikely that the same level of rigour will be applied to capturing lessons, especially when troubleshooting occurs and everyone's attention is on finding a way to just keep moving forward on the critical path.

As the project passes the midway point, we tend to see more consistent efficiency and diminishing returns on the improvement curve. Fewer learnings are captured after each repeated phase, and there is decreasing fluctuation in repeated performances.

Evidencing the value of the improvement process (and the investment in a performance-coaching resource) at the end of a project involves calculating the client-agreed savings from each advance planning meeting, closed and implemented lessons learned, and indeed each implemented suggestion that has typically been prompted by a support initiative and has enabled the team to work smarter (and safer).

The value proposition becomes increasingly clear to existing clients, which is why we often see contract extensions (to support a new scope or new rig); this article is therefore aimed more at potential clients of the performance-coaching service. I hope it encourages you to take the leap of faith and make the investment. The return, according to our clients, is quantifiable and convincing.

CHAPTER 4

WHY DOES MORALE MATTER?

There are three key reasons why morale matters on a performance-improvement campaign:

1. Safety is paramount, and low morale is generally linked to variable concentration and interest levels, which means that the likelihood of a safety incident significantly increases as morale decreases.
2. Energy and productivity are linked to a positive attitude, which itself relies on good morale. By contrast, apathy tends to go hand in hand with

depleted morale, so better morale aligns with better output.

3. Collaboration relies on good team spirit. Team spirit is affected by team morale. Collaboration is essential for effective planning, execution, review, and learning, so without good morale, each of these elements will suffer.

This is a deliberate simplification of a bigger subject, but I hope it conveys the obvious: ignorance of project-team morale is a risk, and ignorance of poor morale is negligent because good morale is essential for safe, productive, and collaborative operations.

We continuously promote a "one team/one mission" ethos on performance-improvement campaigns and our clients regularly feedback that this noticeable impact on team morale is a top-three contributor to project success.

Clearly morale does matter, and we've been privileged to support client leaders in bringing it about on challenging projects involving new teams, new regions, and new rigs. We see it as a critical success factor in any performance-improvement campaign, and to this end, we have evolved our approach to ensure good team morale is always top of mind.

CHAPTER 5

HOW DO WE PAUSE AND STEP BACK IN ORDER TO IMPROVE?

Continuous improvement sounds like a no-brainer, but the reality is that many of us like routine, and we struggle to make smart changes to how we operate.

It is for this very reason that we introduced a WorkSmart initiative as part of our performance-improvement coaching model several years ago. Essentially this initiative invites all members of the project team to articulate work-specific challenges and suggest practical solutions (using a simple WorkSmart card). These suggestions are submitted to the performance coach who records the submissions and then facilitates a regular session with key project leaders in order to focus attention on high-priority improvements that ultimately reduce time and cost, often on the critical path.

Typically, this initiative alone pays for the investment in an experienced and proven external resource to support continuous improvement. The WorkSmart initiative will only gain traction if project personnel feel recognised for their contributions and see their submissions being recorded and progressed. This administrative task requires discipline, diligence, and leadership support.

With the correct approach to enrolment and execution, teams can unleash their potential and make significant improvements in a short space of time. This is exactly what we saw on a two-well drilling campaign last year where the team saved over $1 million by working smarter and safer, not harder. This saving came purely from front-line workers telling their leaders how their jobs could be done better and then having their leaders listen and actually do something about it.

Smart change requires the right appetite for change such that the right people step back and listen to the right ideas. This is easier said than done but a no-brainer once in place.

Let us work smart this year!

CHAPTER 6

HOW DO YOU DIFFERENTIATE AS A PERFORMANCE COACH?

To differentiate as an optional consultant in a project environment, we have always felt it important to demonstrate certain key behaviours so that the team appreciates and understands our role.

As such, we discuss behavioural aspirations which promote this appreciation. Here are ten of the most important:

1. Be positive and avoid negative talk.
2. Look for *what went right* and recognise contributors to the improvement campaign.

3. Demonstrate an exemplary work ethic.
4. Keep your word and do what you say you will.
5. Be situationally aware at all times.
6. Be interested in what others have to say.
7. Embrace diversity and give everyone a voice.
8. Encourage team accountability to stick to our agreements.
9. Be authentic.
10. Be humble.

This is clearly not an exhaustive list, and nor is it always achieved by all coaches at all times on all projects. However, this list provides a foundation for respectful "servant-leadership" on any continuous improvement campaign.

Aspiring to genuinely achieve eight of these ten elements every day will underline your value to project leaders and to the project team. In addition, it will unleash the latent potential of a high-performance team.

> A leader is best when people barely know he exists, when his work is done, his aim fulfilled, they will say: we did it ourselves.
>
> —Lau Tzu

CHAPTER 7

WHY IS IT IMPORTANT TO CONSIDER PROVEN EXTERNAL EXPERTISE?

We are all a function of our upbringings and indeed the environments within which we have worked. Our structure of interpretation (SOI) is based on the reference points we have for how things should be done or, should I say, have been done in our previous experience. In essence, we know what we know, and that is familiar. Familiar is comfortable, so the temptation is to do things the way we have always done them.

Albert Einstein had a well-known quote: "Insanity is doing the same thing over and over again and expecting different results."

Most of us buy into this definition – in theory – and yet it is startling how easily project teams default to "the way it has always been done". This default setting often includes the perspective that no external assistance is needed as "we can manage this in-house". Indeed, this perspective is often underpinned by budget constraints and spending cuts, or leadership insecurity.

The simple truth is that the right external resources will relieve your project team of burdensome administration, whilst also challenging the status quo through recommendation of best practice as measured, and client endorsed, on other successful campaigns.

What price can be placed on time freed up for key project personnel to focus on their core business expertise – without distraction, and on critical path time saved thanks to consistently applied best-practice disciplines to get the best out of the assembled team?

In 2003, Clive Woodward coached England to Rugby World Cup glory in Australia. When interviewed in later years about what contributed to that achievement, Sir Clive often identified the importance of external expertise. His approach was to identify all the components needed to make an athlete or team excel, and then engage the best external resource available to refine each of those components.

A proven expert in continuous improvement through accelerated team-building expertise, and innovative learning know-how, is surely an important consideration if high performance is the aspiration.

CHAPTER 8

WHERE DO THE END USERS SEE THE VALUE WHEN ASKED ABOUT PERFORMANCE COACHING?

Conducting a formal client-feedback process at the end of a performance-improvement intervention of any kind is essential. We have full ISO accreditation and are therefore obliged to request scored feedback from our clients, in addition to written commentary.

Our scored feedback is consistently above eight out of ten, which is humbling. However, it is the end-user comments about where they feel and see the value that helps us understand specifically what is appreciated at the front line.

One of the questions we ask is "what was the most valuable aspect of the service?" The following answers are typical and provide good insight:

1. Disciplined approach to procedural adjustments that removed lost time and cost and enhanced safety during the campaign
2. Engaging all crew to participate in working improvements within a positive and constructive framework
3. Capturing all lessons learned and giving feedback to the crews on their performances
4. Identifying and capturing inefficiencies and then working team solutions before repeating the same activities again made a big difference
5. The way the risk register and lessons-learned tracker have been captured and worked to closure, and are being forwarded to our next campaign, is the most valuable aspect of the service to me

Project sponsors and end users appreciate the opportunity to provide honest feedback. End-user comments are very useful in helping us continually improve the service.

The value is clearly in the simple but essential performance-improvement disciplines of rigorous planning, measuring, and learning, but more than that, the value is perceived in the crew engagement and the team enrolment. "One team, one mission" is key.

We aim to inspire ourselves and the crews with whom we work to unleash our collective potential. We do this with bespoke consulting tools and a servant-leadership approach to the team. We never take clients for granted, and we seek to innovate in accordance to ongoing feedback.

Excellent performance coaching pays for itself many times over. Value, and not cost, is what should be remembered.

CHAPTER 9

WHO CAN BENEFIT FROM PERFORMANCE COACHING?

When you consider that most projects have a combination of people (the wider project team), process (the way the team gets things done), and technology (the equipment necessary to do the work), it is reasonable to suggest that any project can benefit from a coach.

Engaging the right coaching service to support your project is a challenge in itself; the benefits of that engagement will also need to be clear and quantifiable.

The feedback we have had from long-term clients is that there are two key benefits they value when partnering with us:

- A credible and respected coach who can help the team feel like a team before the going gets tough
- Coaching tools which can help the team effectively identify and implement measurable process improvements when the going gets tough

These benefits have been acknowledged by clients dredging for offshore diamonds as well as clients drilling for offshore oil.

Therefore, if you are interested in unleashing the potential of your project team with a "one team/one mission" approach, in accelerating the team building and learning curve using best practice to achieve safer, more-efficient operations at reduced operational cost, leading to earlier production and enhanced company reputation.

If you are keen to mobilise valuable project knowledge from one campaign to the next in order to sustain high performance and to get it right first time in any environment.

If you are part of a committed team with committed leadership, striving to go the extra mile, and achieve the extraordinary, against all odds, you can benefit from performance coaching.

CHAPTER 10

WHAT STIRS YOUR SOUL?

At some point or another, we should all confront the questions "What am I passionate about?", "What makes my heart sing?", and "What work was I born to do?" We reflect on our achievements, our strengths, and ultimately what we are passionate about. Posed another way, we ask, "What inspires me?" and "What stirs my soul?"

A high-performing team is one where all the team members feel that they are drawing on their strengths most of the time each day. It is one where team members feel that they have voices and that their opinions really count. It is also one where team members feel fully enrolled and informed. Stakeholders in the right environment will feel energised to contribute because what they are doing has intrinsic and extrinsic benefit. The narrative is about value not cost. In addition, there is a bond of trust and commitment – true collaboration.

A world-class performance coach helps project leaders create the conditions for this reality: Ideally each specialist should be able to focus on his or her piece of the puzzle, whilst appreciating the bigger picture thanks to clear communication. Supervisors should be inspired to unleash team potential. The continuous-improvement process should become business as usual because it intuitively feels right. Process excellence should be streamlined and driven by a performance coach who clearly loves this aspect of the role. This frees up the enrolled and informed technical experts to focus on their tools and their "turn" on the critical path. Inevitably this leads to better project results.

Joining a new and diverse team with a healthy resistance to change for change's sake, earning my place through congruent service and best-practice facilitation, and then being privileged to join the arduous climb to peak performance, whilst supporting the journey and telling the story along the way, that stirs my soul.

"When you see the view from the top of the mountain, you forget the pain of the climb!"

CHAPTER 11

WHAT ARE SOME EXAMPLES OF MEASURABLE ADDED VALUE FROM PERFORMANCE-IMPROVEMENT CAMPAIGNS?

There is nothing like a simple case study or two to highlight the clear and evident value of a proven and reliable performance-coaching solution which is facilitated by world-class coaches and led by world-class project sponsors and end users.

In 2011 offshore West Africa, the rig team embarked on a managed pressure drilling (MPD) campaign which proved complex and technically challenging. The first time the MPD equipment was rigged up and used, the task took 234 hours. The operation was recorded on video, and a comprehensive review, which captured nineteen key lessons, was conducted by the performance coach.

The second time the task was done, it was performed by an entirely different team, but the edited instructional video was employed, and all nineteen lessons were closed and implemented into the revised procedure. The task took thirty-six hours.

This translated into a saving of eight days, or approximately $6 million.

Another example from offshore South East Asia in 2015 involved the plug-and-abandonment (P&A) phase of a two-well wildcat exploration-drilling campaign: On the first well, there were issues with the cement plugs and with spills of non-spec drilling fluid which resulted in significant lost time and environmental concerns.

More than twenty lessons were documented in a comprehensive review, and the WorkSmart initiative led to various welding tasks which mitigated further spills and improved the flow of fluids. As a result of the improved processes and equipment, the team saved more than three days, or approximately $2 million. More importantly, the environment was better protected thanks to this focus from the team.

Would there have been improvement without a dedicated resource and a specific client-led campaign for accelerated learning? Sure. Would the improvement have been as significant as in these two examples? Unlikely.

Target the value, get the right resources on board, put in the collective effort, and celebrate the results.

CHAPTER 12

HOW IMPORTANT IS IT TO CAPTURE EVERY VALUABLE CONTRIBUTION AT EVERY SIGNIFICANT MEETING?

There is much discussion about the value of a meeting (or meeting too often), but supposing a meeting is agreed as necessary. Then to what degree do you extract every possible ounce of value from that meeting?

"Meeting 101" suggests nominating a chairperson and a scribe, but all too often, neither role is conducted as well as it should be.

The engine of continuous improvement in the offshore-oil-and-gas industry is powered by planning, reviewing, learning, and implementing lessons in time for the repeated task.

As such, the planning meetings, which focus on scrutinisation of the work instructions and agreement of offline preparation activities, are very important and saturated with critical information. The operational reviews are even more important given that their aim is to accurately capture and consider all lessons for subsequent closure.

Central to the value proposition of an expert performance coach in this environment is the disciplined facilitation of planning meetings and operational reviews. More often than not, the coach needs to set the scene for constructive meetings whilst also ensuring that maximum benefit is gained from the congregation of all key stakeholders.

In our experience, with the approval of the team, voice recording of the meetings is the only way to make absolutely sure that no vital nuggets of information go astray. Not only does this allow the performance coach to focus on the team dynamics around the room so that everyone has a voice, but also it means that when the recording is later transcribed, it can be repeatedly replayed to make absolutely sure that crucial detail is checked and understood.

Anything worth doing is worth doing well; the project team relies on a world-class performance coach to ensure that agreed meetings happen, to inspire the right culture at the meetings, and to enable a maximum return on the collective time invested in the get-together.

To add some context, on average, most end users agree that every planning meeting saves an hour of online operational time (>$25,000), and every review captures on average at least three quality lessons (>3 hours or $75,000 saved). Typically, there are about two of each meeting per week, so there is a minimum of $200,000 in team savings every week if meetings are optimised.

Over and above the cost savings, team morale and project safety will benefit from professionally facilitated meetings, which produce valuable output.

In summary, optimising meeting value is potentially the most important aspect of your continuous improvement campaign.

CHAPTER 13

WHAT CAN THE ROYAL MARINES TEACH US ABOUT BUILDING A HIGH-PERFORMANCE TEAM?

Benchmarking the best is always good practice. When it comes to high-performance teams, we don't need to look far beyond the British Commandos. In fact, it was for this very reason that the England Rugby Team sought help from the Corps ahead of their World Cup–winning campaign in 2003.

So what are key elements of Royal Marines' teamwork? What can project teams take away from the elite in order to gain a competitive advantage at the front line?

1. It is a "state of mind": From the outset, the Royal Marines are looking for attitude rather than aptitude.

It is the former that will get you through the tough times, together. We have a quote on the wall here: "Tough times don't last; tough people do."

2. Serving something bigger than each individual: The project identity, legacy, traditions need to unify all team members such that no one man ever becomes bigger than the team or the mission.

3. Core values: The Royal Marines values are excellence, integrity, self-discipline, and humility. Simple explanations are attached to each so that all marines know how to apply these values to daily tasks. The values are tangible.

4. Commando spirit: Courage, determination, unselfishness, cheerfulness; spirit is the X factor, the ethos. It is the non-physical part of a person which is the seat of emotions and character – the soul. Marines aspire to embody these characteristics.

5. Personal and professional development: Royal Marines do not sit still. They are always trying to improve themselves, learn new skills, achieve the next level of capability, and influence in order to be better assets to the team. Each marine and team is trying to be the best they can be.

In summary, the Royal Marines can teach us a huge amount about world-class teamwork: Fundamental to their high performance is a positive mindset, willingly serving the cause, tangible values, commando characteristics, and a tireless pursuit of personal and professional growth.

I was privileged to be part of this extraordinary organisation for eight years. It was an honour to serve, and what I learned about high-performance teams has been invaluable ever since.

CHAPTER 14

WHAT DO WE MEAN BY SERVANT-LEADERSHIP?

There is not much I need to add to the picture of the man: a global inspiration, a national hero, a true legend.

In a world where many are losing faith in government, he was a beacon of hope. His story has understandably been told and retold in every form of media. His vision, his forgiveness, his sacrifice, his integrity, his commitment, his belief in "better", his service to a nation, a continent, and a planet were unique.

He is one of the few irreplaceable mortal role models for servant-leadership; here are three simple points of association we can all use to become better servant-leaders.

1. Be more like Mandela.
2. Earn respect rather than use rank or title; respect is earned in the trenches, and in the board room, by

doing what we say we will and genuinely serving the team and the greater good.

3. Be a role model for others in terms of attitude and impact.

The saying goes, "Reach for the stars. You might not reach them, but at least you'll land on the moon." Mandela leadership is a super-stretch target, but modelling his aura, his approach to earning respect, and his character traits will drive all of us to better servant-leadership.

Thank you, Madiba.

CHAPTER 15

WHAT DO WE MEAN BY AN ACCOUNTABILITY PARTNER?

An accountability partner is a person who coaches another person in terms of helping the other person keep a commitment. This can apply to teams as well as to individuals.

What is performance creep? This happens when standards start to slip over time. An example is a project where the team commits to a review after every operational phase. Perhaps after the third phase, the review does not happen due to a distraction. The next few phases are reviewed as planned, but then several are missed due to other distractions. By the eighth phase, no one is pushing for a review as it feels too much like hard work anyway. Sound familiar?

What about quality versus ticking the box? An example is committing to improve our fitness by going to the gym three times a week. In my experience, there is a big difference between attending a class or using a personal trainer versus training on my own. Class instructors or personal trainers will ensure that I am punctual, prepared, and completely focused.

They also tend to provide motivation and objective feedback! Attending gym ticks the box; optimising my time there assures quality.

A performance coach is an accountability partner. Investing in the right project-performance coach will guarantee the following:

- minimisation or elimination of performance creep
- assured quality versus ticking the box
- motivation and objective feedback

Accelerated improvement is a competitive advantage. An accountability partner will help drive the agreed inputs to achieve extraordinary results earlier than normal. Whether it is cost reduction through smart collaboration or body-fat reduction through smart training, investing in the right accountability partner has proven to yield an exponential return.

CHAPTER 16

WHY HIRE A FACILITATOR FOR YOUR WORKSHOP?

I have this week had the privilege of facilitating a planning workshop for a client based in South Africa but about to commence a significant campaign in Mozambique.

Project teams often wrestle with the question of whether they should manage important workshops internally, or whether they should outsource the facilitation to an external provider.

In the current economic climate, our client was no exception, but having made the decision to invest in external expertise, it is interesting to note the attendant team's feedback on the benefits of their investment. Below is a list of the main points they made.

1. Given the workloads currently faced by key stakeholders, it meant that they did not need to worry about preparation for the workshop, or indeed tracker population and report compilation post workshop – that is all taken care of.

2. Not having to manage the participation and contribution during the sessions enabled the workshop sponsors to fully participate and contribute themselves without worrying about anything else.

3. The external facilitator is unaffected by historical political dynamics within the assembled team. He or she is able to be completely objective throughout.

4. A good facilitator thinks outside the box and innovates a bespoke approach to the gathering based on the specific workshop objectives. The workshop agenda is co-shaped to guarantee leadership enrolment, but a world-class facilitator is obliged to challenge what has been done before and suggest new ways to add value. This was very much the case here as we rolled out a novel "physical-visual" way to highlight risks and key focal points.

5. Their final observation was that excellent facilitation is a skill which is developed like any other skill over many years and many workshops. The cost of all attendees' time for a day away from other operational responsibilities is significant. Surely it makes sense to get maximum return on that time and cost by using someone with the proven skill set to do just that?

Value versus cost should be the clear winner if you have found a quality facilitator for your workshop.

CHAPTER 17

WHAT DO WE MEAN BY CUSTOMER SERVICE?

As a customer yourself, think about what separates an average service provider from an extraordinary one. Now switch to service provider and consider what will ensure prospective clients choose you over anyone else. Furthermore, what would keep them loyal to you over the long term?

In the professional-services sector, where we are always dealing with people, there are certain lessons we have learned about what differentiates outstanding customer service from the also-rans.

1. "Under-promise – over-deliver": This age-old battle cry is still worthy of mention. In simple terms, it is

about exceeding expectations. If we feel we are getting even better value than we paid for, we are generally more than satisfied!

2. "Go the extra mile": Similar but different to the one above, demonstrate at every feasible opportunity that this client relationship is of paramount importance. Often a little more can be done to add value without costing any more money; that little extra every time can lead to a lot more customer loyalty in the longer term.

3. "Practice what we preach": Do what we say we will do, and deliver what we say we will deliver every time. This applies to punctuality, quality, communication, and general behaviour. If we are known to walk the talk and practise what we preach, to look the part and to demonstrate genuine passion for our area of expertise, we will likely gain and retain customers who are disillusioned by the alternative.

The three points above would benefit any relationship, and that is what customer service is about – relationship.

What we mean by customer service is what we mean by exceptional partnership – special treatment as standard.

CHAPTER 18

WHAT DO WE MEAN BY ENTITLEMENT?

Thanks go to Zelim Nel for this article on entitlement.

You've no doubt exercised your mandibles chewing on the benefits and virtues of mental toughness and its foundation-laying role in achieving objectives.

You're well aware that having a strong mental constitution is often the difference between conquering adversity and being conquered by adversity. Having said that, the often overlooked spin-off of such toughness – which runs as a common denominator in all successful journeymen – is a regimented work ethic.

Sport emulates life in most instances, and in the life of a professional athlete, there can be no compromise when it comes to doing the hard yards in preparation for an event.

Such dedication to training is in itself a manifestation of the pillars of mental toughness.

Yet beyond the obvious fruits of regular, committed training sessions (an improvement in fitness, conditioning, and the like) lies a subtler key to success: entitlement.

Jonny Wilkinson was renowned for his kicking sessions. They lasted at least two hours and usually followed a full team practice when his teammates had left for the day. He even practised on Christmas Day, and he's reported to have stayed on the pitch at the end of each session until he was able to split the uprights with twenty consecutive kicks.

This dedication to kicking perfection undeniably improved Wilkinson's physical mechanics, but perhaps more importantly, it gave the England fly-half a sense of entitlement when he stepped up to take an important kick – who could challenge his right to get the next kick over?

Wilkinson was convinced that he deserved to kick accurately. He knew he had prepared extensively for that kick; having kicked the ball thousands of times in practice, he was able to draw on his experience of successfully slotting kicks from similar positions on the field.

This sense of entitlement is a core emotion, and it spawns a deep confidence in athletes.

Mental toughness sets the stage for a commitment to disciplined training, and the application of this work ethic in turn leads to a sense of entitlement.

A legitimate feeling of entitlement is a strong driving force that will not be diverted by anything less than the realisation of your goals.

Practice really does make perfect!

CHAPTER 19

CAN WE AFFORD TO IGNORE
THE BRIGHT IDEAS FROM OUR TEAMS?

When we conducted our usual performance-culture assessment to understand the challenges facing our client in readiness to execute an extremely important completions campaign, we discovered that their lessons-learned register for the two-year drilling campaign contained only 100 lessons and only 25 per cent of those valuable lessons had been closed.

Given the daily project spread cost of that particular operation, this meant that at least $3 million in project savings was sitting unrealised in an Excel file. Understanding this, we can further assume that only a portion of all the genuine lessons and opportunities for improvement had actually been captured in the first place. Conservatively, we can say that there could have been double the number of lessons in the tracker and, therefore, at least another $4 million in unnecessary repeated project costs.

That's $7 million minimum that could potentially have been saved through an under-$1-million investment in an enabled world-class performance coaching solution (coach + tools) to guide robust lesson capture and closure (75 per cent + closure on most projects after three months).

What about the bright ideas that our teams have for working smarter? If lessons are not being rigorously closed due to insufficient internal capacity, then it is a certainty that new ideas generated by team workers at the coal face will not be meticulously harvested, organised, and where appropriate, implemented.

Our clients confirm that the reason for this is that their own teams are already at maximum capacity during the readiness-to-execute and execute phases, working fifteen-hour days and focused on keeping operations moving forward safely.

In the current economic climate with a low oil price and every effort to reduce operating costs, it would seem more important than ever to guarantee the capture and closure of lessons and to inspire the project team to submit regular ideas for additional savings.

This kind of initiative used to be considered optional but must surely now be considered essential: With the best will in the world, technical leaders cannot drive this on their own – they need support for two reasons: (1) the specific skill set required to successfully and continually engage the team on continuous improvement; and (2) the time required to administrate lesson and suggestion registers to the necessary standard for tangible benefit – their focus must be on technical instructions and project leadership – already a full-time job.

Now is the time to promote efficiency and to prevent unnecessary costs. It is time to ensure that the bright ideas from our teams no longer go unattended.

CHAPTER 20

HOW DO WE STAY AHEAD OF THE CURVE?

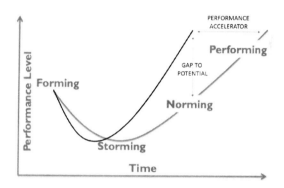

Many of us are familiar with the Tuckman team-growth curve above. This model is accepted as a simple but accurate representation of the stages most teams pass through between formation and high performance.

Many of us are also familiar with the standard time and cost curves by which we track actual performance against planned performance in order to chart how operations are progressing on a project.

To beat normal progress and accelerate to high performance takes something extra. It takes innovation. It takes discipline. It takes leadership.

A proven element of the performance-coaching value proposition is the provision of expertise and experience to unleash the potential of a project team and to accelerate the normal team-growth curve by ensuring that agreed performance-improvement disciplines are uncompromisingly embedded and led from the get-go.

As Einstein said, "Insanity is doing the same thing over and over again and expecting different results." Innovation is now essential for high-performance acceleration; perhaps now is the time to consider accelerating project-team integration in order to stay ahead of the normal performance curve.

CHAPTER 21

HOW DO WE HANDLE PRESSURE WHEN THE PLAN FAILS?

As they say in the military, "No plan survives contact with the enemy."

When performance does not go according to plan, pressure can build. This is when procedures and coping mechanisms are essential.

Pressure equals force divided by area, so one way to manage project pressure is to troubleshoot issues as a team, thus sharing the problem, finding a solution, revising the plan, and moving forward once again.

We work with project teams to ensure that when problems occur, the team takes time to pause, step back, conduct root-cause analysis using a structured approach, and communicate effectively with all key stakeholders to get agreement before moving ahead.

Most of us can relate to the negative manifestation of pressure whereby project leaders can feel compelled to find a quick fix in order to move forward once again. The trouble with this is that the quick fix might briefly mask the root cause which itself will likely recur if not correctly addressed.

One way to handle pressure when the plan fails is to anticipate it, acknowledge it, and then step back, communicate as a team, and identify the true root cause. Facilitated root-cause analysis can help prevent quick fixes and can help build trust. World-class performance coaching incorporates this support and can prove to be a vital resource when the pressure is on.

CHAPTER 22

HOW CAN WE MAINTAIN A HIGH-PERFORMING TEAM IN TIMES OF UNCERTAINTY?

In the oil industry at present, there are many companies struggling as a result of a lower oil price and an unpredictable recovery. The future is uncertain.

At times like these, team members naturally become anxious about their own futures. Morale can suffer as staff search for reassurance and inspiration.

There are some crucial agreements which high-performing project teams have in place in order to drive excellence no matter what the weather outside. These principles should apply anywhere.

1. Meet regularly to maintain clear communication and team unity – meetings need to be short, valuable and well managed with a clear agenda, chairperson, and prompt, actionable output.

2. Measure and display performance – progress against agreed strategic objectives, and actual versus planned performance matters to everyone in the team. Find a way to make it visible even if it is not always positive.

3. Draw on team innovation and creativity to continuously improve – low morale tends to emanate from a sense of disconnect and disempowerment. A sense of contribution and value correlates with higher morale.

4. Recognise team members for a good job well done – look for reasons to praise team members and keep them accurately informed at all times so that they can contribute and respond.

5. Communicate effectively – this is probably the toughest and most important principle to achieve. It involves listening with empathy as well as building trust, yet genuinely effective communication is a competitive advantage in any team!

These principles are woven into our continuous-improvement approach and are especially important during bad weather. We are happy to share examples, and we continue to focus on unleashing the potential of project teams through process discipline and a positive mindset.

CHAPTER 23

WHAT DO WE MEAN BY A LEAP OF FAITH?

Sometimes in business and in life, we simply have to consider the evidence, weigh up the pros and cons, and then take a leap of faith.

Gut feel plays a role, and indeed, our attitudes will often dictate how our decisions play out.

It is like this with coaching. There will be evidence of the impact coaching has had elsewhere. There will also be positive and negative commentary based on different experiences and perspectives.

Ultimately, the investment decision will be a leap of faith, but with sound research, a considered choice of coach, and commitment to the process, our client feedback has repeatedly shown this to be a very rewarding investment well made.

Growth requires a paradigm shift. A step change in performance inevitably requires a new approach and, to some extent, a leap of faith.

CHAPTER 24

WHAT CAN CROSSFIT TEACH US ABOUT CONTINUOUS IMPROVEMENT?

CrossFit does not appeal to everyone, but in fairness, most forms of physical endeavour provide similar lessons to business and life.

My experience with CrossFit is that there are definitely some key elements of the general culture and approach which have transferable value for continuous-improvement campaigns in any setting.

1. The most significant element is the sense of community which is built upon a shared passion and commitment to get better through determination and perseverance. More than that, there is a real focus on listening and

learning from each other based on different techniques and personal triumphs over adversity.

2. Most CrossFit boxes have their rules somewhere visible; these include two very relevant points for aspirant champions: (a) leave your ego at the door; and (b) always be on time. At the top level in this sport, there is a genuine humility and discipline which inspires the average enthusiast to strive for improvement.

3. What gets measured gets managed. There is a genuine attention to data and detail in CrossFit; numerous apps have emerged over the last year which enable easy mobile capture and analysis of each workout so that comparison can be made with peers and personal history. Data analysis drives planning and programming while workout reviews contribute more data – this in turn drives quantifiable continuous improvement.

4. Encouragement and recognition, where needed and where it is due, become second nature because it is the right thing to do. Fitter, faster athletes make a point of cheering on less experienced enthusiasts as a matter of course. This engenders a sense of confidence, trust, and mutual respect throughout the community.

5. Everyone clears up after themselves no matter who they are. There is a real sense that every member of the community contributes to the quality of the experience and the workout environment. This attitude and action is led by the coaches. It underscores the fact that no matter how fit the athlete, the box is bigger than any individual.

There are clearly some very transferable lessons from CrossFit to continuous improvement campaigns in general: create a community, drop the ego and be punctual, measure performance, encourage and recognise others, and serve the community to make it better!

CHAPTER 25

HOW DO WE ACHIEVE A > 50:1 ROI THROUGH PERFORMANCE COACHING?

We recently stepped away from a rig project we supported for over four years.

Thanks to the project team's commitment to an accelerated and ongoing improvement campaign, in excess of $275 million was saved during that time.

We asked the end users what they believed contributed most significantly to this achievement. Their feedback was as follows:

- Exceptional leadership on and offshore to understand and utilise the coaching resource to its full potential.

- Advance planning meetings taking place without fail, for every major operational phase, and being run properly with all offline activities minuted and chased before commencement on the critical path.
- All lessons captured and rigorously analysed through to solution and implementation or to rejection so that mistakes are not repeated and improvements are inserted into forward plans as soon as possible.

The breakdown of the financial benefits was $160 million saved against operational budget, $110 million in implemented team learnings, and close to $5 million in implemented team suggestions through our WorkSmart initiative.

The safety benefit was over one thousand days without a lost-time incident.

The rig benefit was moving from last place 2012 to first in the regional fleet in 2015.

We have trained and mentored internal resources to continue the improvement process; the big challenge for them will be to maintain objectivity. But leaving behind sustainable internal capability is a fundamental component of any coaching contract, so this element is vital.

In summary, performance coaching has proven in this case to have provided a massive return on the overall investment. There would, however, have been zero return if the client leadership team had been uninformed and unenrolled. Furthermore, there would have been limited benefit without an uncompromising team commitment to well organised operational-planning meetings and the focused closure of lessons learned.

Provided strong leadership is in place, and the benefit of external performance coaching is understood and supported, the cost concern disappears.

CHAPTER 26

WHAT DO WE MEAN BY PERFORMANCE DISRUPTION?

The word *disruption* seems to be increasing in popularity. Recently it has been frequently used in the context of business and innovation.

It got me thinking about the concept and whether I could find a clear example of the impact of disruption. Let's start with a business definition: "to change the traditional way that something is done, especially in a new and effective way".

There is an excellent example from sport. Consider the high jump in track and field. For over half a century, the "roll" or "straddle" method was used, partly because jumpers were not landing on a foam mat in the early days, but in 1968, Dick Fosbury came up with the "Fosbury Flop," clearing the bar backwards rather than forwards. It completely changed the way high jump was done, and it spiked performance over the next decade. Between 1920 and 1968, the world record had improved by 15 cm. In the next ten years it had improved by the same height again! The Fosbury Flop is now the standard.

Disruption apparently transcends innovation in that the latter tends to build on existing trends while disruption can be unpredicted and unexpected whilst often causing a massive paradigm shift.

I then got to thinking about the performance-coaching approach we have taken with clients and whether any of our embedded interventions have been truly disruptive. Difficult to tell for sure, but certainly one element of our toolkit, which aligns to the definition of "change in tradition + new and effective", is the use of video and the building of a project video library for all operational sections, including key steps and lessons learned, in order to help project personnel to visualise safe, best practice, and teamwork.

We introduced this as one of our performance solutions on a deep-water drill ship in 2008–2009, and whilst there was initial scepticism and surprise from some, there was also a measurable impact on safety and operational performance.

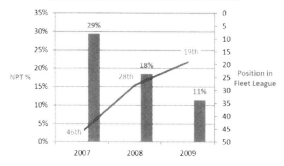

CONTINUOUS IMPROVEMENT EXPLORED

For this client, performance coaching was certainly a beneficial innovation with significant gains through proven best practice such as facilitated planning and review.

Arguably the disruption, which created a step change in front-line performance, came in the form of edited videos for all operations, including translated-text annotation for key lessons learned. Visualisation removed the language barrier, so crews collaborated with confidence and productive time increased by 18 per cent! This rig had never had an operational video library before.

A project video library for accelerated performance improvement is now a standard spoke in our transformation wheel, a disruptive "Fosbury Flop"!

CHAPTER 27

HOW DO WE GO THE EXTRA MILE?

Going the extra mile is often the difference between good and great, between competing and winning.

Performance coaches need to understand how to promote a culture in which "extra-mile" best practice is normal practice. In other words, how to create a twenty-seven-mile marathon as standard.

Here are my four takeaways from direct experience working in four different industries, which can help us go the extra mile as standard:

1. Sport: Develop a positive mental attitude (PMA) and build resilience.
    Perspective – turn adversity into competitive advantage.
    Clear process goals – focus on what we can control.
    A strong bench – build a squad with depth.

2. Oil and Gas: Apply best practice at all times, no matter what.
    Advance planning and after-action review for every operation
    Lessons learned and WorkSmart ideas pursued to implementation
    Recognition and morale treated as priority

3. Military: Be prepared for the unexpected – hope for the best; train for the worst.
    Tactical aide-memoire – checklists for reference and best options
    Drills and exercises to stay battle ready at all times
    War gaming – get used to thinking/delivering under pressure.

4. Corporate: Prioritise your people at all times – engagement, empowerment, enrolment for extra-mile commitment
    It starts and ends with servant-leadership.
    Agree your values and then practise those values.
    Embrace the diversity of the team.

In summary, going the extra mile is by definition a challenging task. It takes extra effort, extra heart, and extra will. It also leads to extraordinary results. The takeaways highlighted above can help get us there: positive mental attitude, non-negotiable best practice, expecting the unexpected, and prioritising our people at all times. There is very little traffic on the extra mile – most teams don't get that far.

CHAPTER 28

WHAT CAN WE LEARN FROM THE ALL BLACKS LEGACY?

In the context of performance, we cannot ignore the most successful sports team of all time. The All Blacks have a win rate of 78 per cent but 84 per cent since the game went professional and 93 per cent in the last five years!

There are as many reasons why other countries should be better than New Zealand as there are superlatives to describe the class of their rugby. Yet they continue to dominate in a way which very few other teams of any type can emulate.

The book *Legacy* by James Kerr explores and unpacks fifteen themes which differentiate the All Blacks and provide lessons in leadership for anyone willing to learn. It is one of the best books I have ever read.

I will go with my gut on the three most aspirational and transformational components of the All Black legacy from a high-performance perspective, three boosters for an unstoppable force.

1. "Haka" – All rugby followers enjoy watching the haka before a test match. The Maori battlefield war cry is fixating, and for All Black opposition, it must be hugely intimidating. But more than that, I think what project teams can take from the traditional haka is the significance of the investment made in a ritual which has nothing to do with the specific technical skills required to win the rugby match.

   There is no doubt that the haka gives the All Blacks a competitive advantage despite the fact that it does not involve a rugby ball, a pass, a kick, or a tackle. The haka clearly enables incredible intangible integrity; it builds up the team to be truly greater than the sum of its parts. It inspires collective self-belief, fearlessness, and camaraderie. It is about identity, unity, history, legacy.

2. Continuity – Succession planning in the All Blacks has become world class since the beginning of the professional era. There seems to be an instinctive mentorship programme whereby older players and former players fiercely protect the All Black brand and ensure that younger players entering the fray are inducted into this vital mindset: Players are required to leave the jersey in a better place than when they received it.

For project teams, the aspiration is surely to inspire experienced campaigners to mentor and model the requisite approach to achieve the best possible results so that younger team members understand and revere the expectation from the get-go.

3. Stamina – A signature of many All Blacks victories is the scoring of points late in the game to secure the win. They have a renowned "finish-strong" mentality. There are games where the All Blacks have displayed remarkable composure and concentration to string upwards of twenty phases together before crossing the chalk for an injury-time try. The point is that they clearly train stamina as a genuine competitive edge. When other teams are tiring or quitting, the All Blacks are shifting into top gear.

If project teams can use relevant training and experience to promote team stamina, they too can go the extra mile as standard in order to win more and fulfil latent potential.

In summary, the All Blacks clearly epitomise high performance, so it is worth studying them and adopting transferable elements to improve project teams. They unleash true potential through a unique identity which is held in the highest regard and passed on from one generation to the next. They also have a specific focus on stamina to finish stronger than all the competition and to get the job done.

I'm a diehard Green and Gold Springbok supporter, but there is no doubt the benchmark is All Black.

CHAPTER 29

WHAT WERE SOME OF THE KEY MESSAGES FROM LEADERCAST 2016?

I was lucky enough to speak at Leadercast Aberdeen earlier this year. After my speaking part, I tuned into the speakers from the United States and noted some excellent observations which apply as much to personal leadership as brand leadership. I re-read my notes recently and was reminded of some of the valuable takeaways for individuals, coaches, and business teams.

1. Clarity – is it absolutely crystal clear what you stand for and what you mean? A great way to lose credibility is to create confusion about our purpose. We should be associated with reliability and consistency rather than mixed messaging and double standards. Clear equals simple equals memorable, and memorable is portable.
   Create a clear vision that people believe in.

2. Situational awareness – how do people experience you, and how do people experience themselves in your presence? This skill requires constant effort to improve, and yet it is often paid mere lip service.

Adjusting to different cultures and cues is a subtle art but immensely significant in the context of our potential impact as leaders. Having created a clear vision, we now need to reinforce the behaviour that's aligned with that shared vision.

Model consistently what we want to see in others.

3. Do the right thing – focus on the right thing and impact everything. As leaders we have an obligation to make things better even though things could be worse. In order to be the best we can be as individuals or as teams, leadership requires decision making and this can separate good from great. It is the right way, rather than the easy way that wins hearts, minds and campaigns. Where needed, provide the skills to break new ground.

Keep ourselves and the team moving forward.

In summary, be crystal clear, be situationally aware, and always strive to do the right thing to keep moving forward. Lead on.

CHAPTER 30

WHAT CAN WE LEARN FROM THE OLYMPICS?

Every four years we are reminded of what is humanly possible. We are inspired by feats of heroism and athleticism that transcend the extraordinary. But the most amazing aspect of this sporting spectacle is that, for the most part, these feats are achieved by "ordinary-looking" people.

If you lined up ten amateur sportsmen, you couldn't necessarily pick out the Olympian simply by physical appearance. Of course this applies to some sports more than others, but the point is made: It is what you don't see that has the biggest impact on performance, even at the Olympic level!

We are talking about positive mindset – commitment, discipline, self-belief, determination. This can turn ordinary into extraordinary; in skilled athletes and Olympic teams with visionary leadership and world-class coaching, this turns to gold.

Champion project teams can learn from this: Assembling the right people with the right skills is essential, and strong leadership is key, but inspiring the Olympic mindset will get us over the line in record time.

The Para-Olympics promotes this point to a whole new level; impossible is nothing as they say.

So what can we learn from the Olympics? Probably a number of lessons, but the most obvious to me is this; we are all capable of so much more.

CHAPTER 31

HOW DOES PERFORMANCE COACHING ENABLE SAFER OPERATIONS?

Bill Robb from Safety Improvers recently posted about the "behavioural traps that lead people to make decisions that lead to actions that result in people being hurt". Bill is a leading expert on the subject of safety, and this was yet another excellent article from him.

All operations should prioritise safety above everything else, and my aim with this article is to underline how performance coaching ensures that the safety agenda is indeed above the rest.

Performance coaches are a team resource focused on the implementation and uncompromising maintenance of project disciplines which mitigate Bill's identified behavioural traps below:

> Fear of perceived leadership and peer pressure – a way to allay this fear is by constantly acknowledging the issue and consistently promoting an empowered culture whereby everyone feels comfortable to stop the job if something feels or looks dangerous. This acknowledgement and promotion is done at well-facilitated operational-planning-and-review meetings where safety and operational leaders, and any other team members, are able to effectively communicate expectations. Good performance coaches should be at the centre of these sessions to ensure that everyone has a voice.

> Lack of awareness – a way to build awareness is by working tirelessly to ensure key information is visible, accessible, understandable, and transferable. Verbal communication is essential, but this can be complemented by poster campaigns, video messages, and, of course, other digital media. Good performance coaches should have the necessary skills and accountability to enable exceptional awareness.

> Loss of concentration – a way to maintain concentration is by inspiring a high-performance team with a strong work ethic and a strong sense of loyalty and accountability between all team members. Toolbox talks immediately before a task should focus everyone, but ultimately, the culture will drive consistently high levels of concentration. Good performance coaches

play a major role in establishing the right team culture for the safe achievement of all objectives.

Inaccurate risk assessment – there are no short cuts to the comprehensive interrogation of project risk; a user-friendly but robust risk register is necessary pre-execution to ensure that all risks identified at the key-risk-awareness sessions are captured, extensively discussed by experienced subject-matter experts, and mitigated to the greatest degree possible. This detail can then be filtered according to forthcoming tasks and included in planning meetings so that risks are clearly understood and addressed on the rig floor prior to execution. Good performance coaches have the tools and the responsibility to support safety leaders in keeping risk assessment and awareness at the forefront of the collective mind at all times.

Bill Robb highlights the importance of coaching and discipline to tackle human factors and enable safer operations. Performance coaches, who are sought out for their positive impact, will drive the agreed performance-improvement disciplines and engage with the workforce to help keep the team as safe as possible. High-performing teams are safe teams. Thanks for your insights, Bill.

CHAPTER 32

HOW DO WE BUILD A WORLD-CLASS TEAM?

Like many people, I have been involved in team building for a long time, initially at school, learning how to get the best out of our boarding house, track relay, and rugby teams; then in the marines, learning how to unite warriors behind a mission; in the corporate world as a workshop facilitator; and finally in the oil industry, striving for the secret to team success as both a project manager and performance coach.

I have been searching for the key ingredients of a high-performing team, and whilst I will not claim to have found the perfect recipe, I will say that by reflecting on one other (much more significant) learning experience, I feel a breakthrough coming on. I'm talking about *family*!

Being a child and sibling growing up, I had some appreciation of teamwork to get things done. As a co-parent of three young kids, I now have a crystal-clear insight into the difference between average and amazing family-work: In a genetic family environment, when all family members discuss and truly collaborate to successfully implement a plan, the sense of satisfaction is immense. When this family teamwork is performed under pressure against a threatening challenge, the bond becomes primal.

Maybe this is why elite professionals who are part of world-class teams, talk about their community as family. It is effectively the highest honour that can be given to a generic team – brothers in arms, band of brothers, #blood #family.

If we accept then that special team communities aspire to become a family, we need to explore what makes a special family. In theory if we understand this, we may have the key to unlocking world-class teamwork. We'll focus here on five key contributing steps to becoming a super family.

1. Sacrifice – this speaks for itself and, in one word, provides a perfect anchor for family actualisation. Parents and children in any functioning family understand that there is more than just themselves to think about. This means compromising on the personal wish list and involves serving other family members to maintain overall progress.

2. Support – the stronger the mutual support in the family, the greater the chances of family security and future growth. Being there for each other and particularly parents being there for their children, is the foundation of trust, loyalty and integrity.

3. Stability – a confident family unit is built on a stable platform, an island of calm even when the surrounding

seas might be somewhat rough. This requires reliable, accountable family members and a familiar home base. It enables identity.

4. Systems – spontaneity is important, but there must be a fundamental set of guidelines and principles from which the family operates. This provides structure. Routines and checklists are generally followed as standard.

5. Success – this can be measured in many different ways, but it is vital for morale and for momentum. Celebrating success is central to a happy family, and members are motivated to achieve more based on how they see success benefiting the family unit.

World-class teamwork is indeed a lofty goal. It continues to be the focus for millions of people and billions of dollars. There are thousands of books on the subject. Potentially it is naïve to try and simplify the concept, but I am certain that top teams talk about being a family, and family undoubtedly benefits from the 5 S's listed above.

Reunions and relationships forged during tough team campaigns bear out the link. From team formation to "family" status can be a very long journey, but the steps above at least provide a start.

CHAPTER 33

WHAT IS THE ELEPHANT IN THE ROOM?

Imagery is powerful. One of my favourite metaphors is the elephant in the room.

Similes are also valuable; one of our current clients describes the performance-coaching service as "cheap as chips" based on the cost savings realised through a structured learning process which is managed by a dedicated resource. In his opinion, the team safety and savings through accelerated improvement render the service cost irrelevant.

Analogies are extremely useful; they are effectively a comparison between one thing and another, typically for the purpose of explanation or clarification.

I find myself constantly searching for analogies to help naysayers understand the value of coaching. One of my favourites is the GPS and map analogy: We can plug a post code into a GPS and follow instructions to get us to a destination. That is fine. We do it often. But if there comes a time when there is either no address or no GPS, and we have not invested time in understanding how to read a map, we will be lost. Coaches help us learn to navigate our own way rather than relying on someone else for the answer. This builds internal capacity. It generates self-improvement. It unleashes latent potential. In short, coaching enables individuals and teams to drive better results for themselves – this is reinforced by commentary from uber-successful entrepreneurs like Bill Gates.

Performance coaching in the context of the energy sector, where we have delivered the service predominantly in oil and gas, is all about providing a structure and a toolkit which helps the teams we support to become the best they can, as soon as they can.

One of the oldest but best performance-coaching analogies I have come across is the comparison to personal fitness training, either in a one-on-one or a class-training setup. Admittedly, the fact that clients are following instructions from the "coach" means it is slightly different to the oil-and-gas-project coaching context; however, the elements of accountability partnership, process discipline and process goals, planning and review, tracking and recording progress, and attitude role modelling are all analogous.

Most people I have asked about using a personal trainer have said there is no way they would have achieved even half of what they have without a specialist accountability partner who ensures that the agreed process is rigorously followed, and that performance progress is tracked and visible. There is an investment in an optional service with results that are exponentially better than if the individual or team went without focused and specialist support: cost forgotten, benefit tangible and measurable.

Another great analogy for me is learning a new language; assuming it is optional but potentially highly valuable (travelling and possibly working in another country), there is significant similarity there. Assuming there is a cost for the language coach, then that is similar. The coach or tutor will bring structure and a toolkit to accelerate learning and group work (if there is a class group), but ultimately the student or students will have to engage and commit (ownership, process, time) in order to realise course success. Once the language is learned, the coach can step away; the client is now independent and far more capable, more confident, and more effective (for the long term). The return on initial investment is likely to be measurable and significant in terms of time and money saved through enhanced capability and efficiency: cost forgotten, benefit overwhelming.

More often than not, performance coaches just help us do what we could do on our own but don't. What price should we put on a resource that helps us genuinely exceed our expectations and unleash our potential?

So what is the elephant in the room? There needs to be a project, ideally over six months in duration; there needs to be a real appetite for excellence from the leadership team; and the project needs the right performance coach. With that, I completely agree.

CHAPTER 34

WHY CAN WE ALL RELATE TO ROCKY?

Everyone loves an underdog. The Rocky Balboa story appeals to everyone because we all face adversity at some time or another, and we seek inspiration to turn things around and to triumph against the odds.

All champions have had to fight through personal or public doubt. The few minutes of podium glory are built on years of sacrifice and hard work.

The Rocky film series was inspired by a real boxer, a relative unknown who went nearly fifteen rounds with the great Muhammad Ali.

Project teams are made up of many inexperienced and often unknown personnel. Teams are required to step into the proverbial ring and take on whatever challenges are thrown at them.

To become a champion team means that ordinary people need to achieve the extraordinary together. Many teams fail just like many underdogs merely make up the numbers. So what is the most important lesson we can learn from Rocky when it comes to reaching the top of the steps?

For me the answer has to be desire – a burning, inextinguishable desire to prove what is possible when you set your mind to it. Achieving collective desire in a new project team requires careful leadership and organisation. We call it "one team, one mission" and have an initial step in our approach which focuses on building team identity and inducting project members into the fold.

I'm reminded of one of my favourite quotes from Mark Twain: "It's not the size of the dog in the fight; it's the size of the fight in the dog." The underdog with the inextinguishable desire to fight through adversity and emerge unconquered at the top of the steps. Thanks for the inspiration Rocky.

CHAPTER 35

WHY PROMOTE INDIVIDUAL STRENGTHS?

I am a big fan of the quote "Everybody is a genius. But if you judge a fish by its ability to climb a tree, it will live its whole life believing that it is stupid."

We all have strengths and weaknesses. The founder of CrossFit, Greg Glassman, is quoted as saying, "Hiding from your weaknesses is a recipe for incapacity and error." I think this is also an important point, especially in the context of physical fitness.

My view, therefore, is that a project team will deliver best results if the individuals within the team are in positions which draw on their demonstrated and appreciated strengths, *and* those same individuals are continually striving to improve themselves, including awareness of and attention to personal weaknesses.

When I completed my full-time MBA at the Graduate School of Business (GSB) in Cape Town 2001, I was part of a syndicate of about eight students throughout the year; halfway through the year, the syndicates were reshuffled in order to change the dynamics and force new collaboration. In the first instance, we were a dysfunctional team and failed to divide tasks according to individual strengths; in the second syndicate group we were much more effective at ensuring that we allocated and accepted work in accordance with our interests and experience. My first syndicate consistently propped up the bottom of the academic tables, while my second was consistently towards the top. There was an element of general learning and improvement throughout the student body, but there was also a specific focus in our second group on leveraging the individual strengths available. The impact was measurable and unquestionable.

I was subsequently involved in designing and overseeing an annual breakaway for the new MBA syndicates of the full- and part-time GSB programmes. Our aim was to compress and accelerate the natural team-building curve by putting the groups under different types of pressure in a fun outdoor environment, and providing multiple reference points for dynamic awareness and integration so that syndicates commenced the academic curriculum as an established team, aware of individual strengths, and beyond the issues that often delay constructive bonding. The GSB has seen a noticeable drop in syndicate dysfunction as a result of this continued annual initiative. Students have responded that they feel the upfront breakaway eradicates ego and posturing and reveals individual strengths and weaknesses within hours. This is then a springboard to team effectiveness, enjoyment, and the smart division of tasks.

Understanding and promoting individual strengths within a project team tends to lead to harmony and high performance. There are many tools available to identify individual strengths, and the right one for your team is probably a smart investment.

Perhaps the author of the quote was suggesting that we measure team members against agreed goals which align with their interests and strengths. How hard can it be?

CHAPTER 36

WHAT DO WE MEAN BY MENTAL TOUGHNESS?

Different examples come to mind for different people when you hear the phrase "mental toughness". One thing is for sure: the influence our minds have on our performances cannot be underestimated.

A great mental-toughness analogy I have heard before relates to a car dashboard fuel gauge. The body wants to stop working when the indicator reaches the red line; the mind, however, knows that there is another 10 per cent left in the tank. If our minds are strong enough to keep our bodies going, it is a 10 per cent competitive advantage!

Mental toughness is also about keeping an ice-cool head during the intense heat of battle. One of my mentors, Steve Harris, used to talk about "fire and ice", and he developed a structured approach to building mentally tough rugby players when he and I were working with the future stars of South African rugby more than ten years ago. Together, we created workshops and breakaways for professional teams, which integrated mental-toughness theory with practical challenges to illustrate and manifest the benefit of enhanced mental skills.

In my own experience as a commando, captain, CrossFitter, and coach, there are four trigger statements which best exemplify mental toughness for me.

1. Expect the unexpected: As a marine, this was a phrase with which I became well acquainted. It becomes a mindset. By subconsciously planning for the worst, it is always a bonus if the worst does not occur. An outcome different to what was expected, if not the worst possible outcome (someone died), is still not as bad as it could have been and, therefore, a bonus! Improvise, adapt, overcome is what commandos are taught. The circumstances have changed, it was unexpected, but we need to crack on. Embrace this attitude, and we'll be on our way to mentally tough.

2. Finish strong: This became my rallying cry as a leader of teams in sports as wide-ranging as rugby and adventure racing. I now apply it on projects with our coaching teams. The temptation is for our effort level to drop as we approach the end of a challenge. It is all too easy to coast in to the finish line, especially if those around us are doing the same. But if we make it a habit to accelerate rather than brake around the final

bend, it will become second nature and will override the "quit button" when the going gets really tough.

3. Compete every workout of the day (WOD): I got into CrossFit four years ago. At a stage when I was finding the gym somewhat monotonous, it was exactly what I needed, and I have never looked back. That said, high-intensity workouts are not for the faint of heart, and the few competitions I have attended can brutally expose poor technique or a weak engine if you are not fully prepared. This year I decided to make a step change mentally; I treat every training WOD as if a competition, and as a result, I am less and less intimidated by competition or new exercise combinations – it becomes business as usual no matter how big the stage. Physically I am getting fitter, but mentally, I am tougher as well.

4. Focus on process: This point has been reiterated to me a few times in recent autobiographies and articles I have read. If you attach success to outcomes and you fail to achieve these, you feel like a failure. If you attach success to process, you build confidence provided you commit. The process is completely owned by us and is not subject to forces outside our control (which is the case with outcomes). However, if the process or training program has been carefully designed to achieve best possible improvement, the outcomes will follow. Confidence is a key mental skill, so an increase in this means a tougher mind overall.

In each of the four areas above, rebounding from failure and maintaining resilience in adversity has been key. Never give up. This is important in the context of individual and team performance where setbacks can seem terminal, yet once overcome, they are simply lessons learned.

Much has been written about mental toughness, and there are many different opinions on the subject. My aim with this brief article is simply to provoke thought and to reflect on my own reference points using four trigger statements which sustain my mental game on every project. Expect the unexpected, always finish strong, train hard, and focus on the process: this combination has enabled me to face down a few giants in my time.

CHAPTER 37

WHAT DO WE MEAN BY MARGINAL GAINS TO STEP CHANGE?

Most of us are aware of the four-minute mile and the fact that no one in the world of track and field believed the four-minute barrier could be broken before Bannister achieved this feat in 1954.

The sub-four-minute mile represents a step change in the history of middle-distance running. The record stood at 4:01 for nine years, and yet once Bannister had broken the barrier, it was broken again within 9 weeks!

It took many years for Bannister to create this step change in athletic perception. This was done through marginal gains as illustrated below.

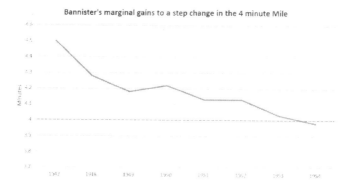

Bannister's marginal gains to a step change in the 4 minute Mile

Not only did he demonstrate continuous improvement (with a few setbacks), but also he demonstrated what we now call marginal gains by targeting minutiae such as lighter running shoes and sharper spikes as well as innovative training techniques, such as fartlek and interval running.

Dave Brailsford, the GB cycling-performance director, recently popularised the concept of "marginal gains" and how he targeted 1 per cent improvements in everything that had even the slightest impact on a cyclist's performance in order to achieve the breakthroughs we have witnessed over the last five years in British cycling. He cited examples as random as better handwashing to prevent illness and consistent pillows for sleeping to emphasise the point that every tiny change for the better will potentially underpin a genuine step change in performance come the day of the race.

As a project performance coach, I find this most illuminating and a strong reminder that behavioural habits and process disciplines under our control are the strongest levers to achieve project success. We continually evolve our transformation methodology to cover all bases for incremental wins, no matter how small.

Tim Wigham

Marginal gains often seem irrelevant at the time, yet in hindsight, their contribution to the ultimate step change in perception and performance can be fundamental.

Capturing one lesson and making one safety observation a day on an oil rig can feel like a very marginal gain, yet we've seen this contribution scale up over a short time, and when every crew member is capturing a lesson and making an observation, a performance step change can be achieved. The micro gains take some sacrifice and extra effort; the step change in performance makes it all worthwhile.

CHAPTER 38

WHAT DO WE MEAN BY ROI?

I am currently immersed in a performance-culture assessment for the operational division of an oil-and-gas company. The assessment allows us to listen to those who are actually making things happen at the front line; we learn about the challenges they face, we ask about what could improve, we respect and collate the feedback to our structured questions, and we get a sense of the current reality for each project team.

In addition, we ask key stakeholders about their desired futures. We note the differences of opinion so that any misalignment can be addressed and debated through to an agreement on mission, vision, goals, and measures of success.

Without a performance-culture assessment, there is insufficient reconnaissance to ensure that an approved coaching intervention is laser-focused on the right areas to get the maximum return on effort.

A performance-improvement campaign can transform project performance from the current reality with all of its challenges and failings to a desired future which typically includes safe, profitable operations, achieving agreed objectives whilst maintaining team morale and rewarding individual commitment and contribution.

It all sounds simple and straightforward, but without a long-term transformation commitment from project leadership, the future reality will continue to be the current reality. Furthermore, transformation takes time; the return on the investment of money, energy, and effort will not be immediately apparent. Indeed, it will not materialise if the proven steps to genuine change, and specific priorities for each project team, are not addressed with uncompromising discipline.

The immediate priorities are also known as the low-hanging fruit. For us, these priorities are typically the most tangible improvements to enrol the front-line workforce to enable some early "wins" and to launch the transformation process. An example priority is either of the foundational layers of Maslow's hierarchy of human needs (welfare and/or safety). If there is a clear issue here, it needs to be resolved before further progress can be made.

I am passionate about unleashing the potential of a project team and about helping the team to influence what they can in order to give high performance the best possible chance of success. This is why I do what I do.

In the commercial world, there is a very necessary focus on ROI, or return on investment. An investor in a product or service must be convinced that the return justifies and ideally multiplies the investment – proven value-add.

In today's world of instant gratification, it can sometimes be difficult to persuade investors that transformation can take time to achieve. I was inspired recently during this assessment when a key-rig site supervisor talked about the absolute necessity to focus on team first – safety, ownership, initiative, community spirit. While he was talking, I noticed a recently printed chart which showed that on a key divisional operational measurable, he had the best-performing team. No coincidence, I thought. A genuine leadership investment in safety, teamwork, and process compliance had led to a best-in-class result after a year of hard work. In his words, "We didn't change any equipment; we changed our mindset." I learned that the team had gone from last to first.

With people and process, transformation takes time. It takes world-class leadership and team enrolment, commitment, consistency, and ongoing effort. However, we have seen time and again that provided leaders have the strength and vision, provided the right team is on/in the field; and provided the right steps are followed with uncompromising discipline, the ROI is the desired future. Simple as that.

CHAPTER 39

WHAT IS THE VALUE OF VIDEO FOR CONTINUOUS IMPROVEMENT?

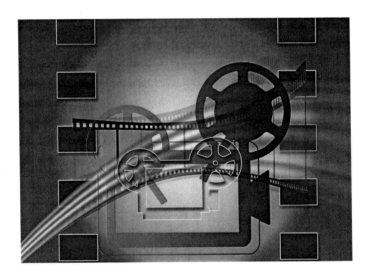

Video has been around for a long time now, and with digital disruption in full force, it is certainly not a novelty. In this day and age, videos are super easy to create, edit, produce, and send. Yet the use of video to support performance improvement in heavy-industry operational environments is far from established.

My colleague Steve Blades introduced me to the concept of moviemaking as a fun, interactive, and genuinely beneficial event for corporate team building in South Africa twelve years ago. I subsequently used it for group dynamics during executive breakaways and then introduced it to the deep-water offshore-drilling world as a crucial spoke in our continuous-learning-and-improvement wheel back in 2008.

Explaining the value of video has become easier thanks to the various video channels on YouTube, for example Food Tube, which is an online search-friendly instructional video recipe library which enables kitchen cavemen like me to learn how to cook an omelette! The point is that you can search for the recipe you need, and you can then watch the process evolve with verbal instructions, clear visuals, and best of all, the ability to pause or rewind as needed.

The very same principle can be applied to upstream oil-and-gas operations. We have successfully built up rig-based video libraries on behalf of our clients so that all operations, inductions, drills, and celebrated achievements are captured to enhance learning, performance, consistency, and morale. Operational-section videos can be particularly valuable for inexperienced crews or front-line supervisors who have not done that particular phase for a long time.

Playing a comprehensive operational-phase video, with either soundtrack or voice-over, along with annotated commentary – translated as necessary – ahead of the same forthcoming operational phase, subliminally prepares crew for what they will see and do. It mentally prepares operators for what to expect in the very same way that a safety video prepares passengers for a helicopter flight offshore.

We place such significance on this element of our continuous improvement toolkit because of the positive feedback we have received from our clients.

If a picture paints a thousand words, how many more a video? It is of course essential that videos receive oversight and expert quality assurance as well as accurate annotation. This

Tim Wigham

is where coaching expertise is required so that all parties are enrolled and involved in the initiative.

Provided this is professionally done, the value of video for continuous improvement is extraordinary: visually inducting crew into the safety culture saves lives; seeing what is happening helps the engineering team make million-dollar decisions; seeing how a job is done helps the drill crew save hours through learning, preparation, awareness, and efficiency; enabling workers to show their loved ones what they do and where they work boosts recognition and morale.

Safer, smarter, more-efficient operations, performed by a more motivated workforce, sounds like a reasonable value proposition. As part of a suite of tools designed to accelerate improvement on any project—no brainer.

CHAPTER 40

BATTLEFIELD TO OILFIELD

In many parts of the world, oil goes hand in hand with instability and conflict. Fighting to secure control of significant oil reserves is a familiar story. Indeed, the oilfield has effectively been a battlefield in many regions for many decades.

There are other parallels too; a small percentage of oilfield workers have done some time on a battlefield somewhere. The work environment appeals: geographic frontiers, high-cost, high-risk operations requiring resourcefulness, leadership, teamwork, and perseverance to succeed.

Currently there are many oil companies battling to survive. The oversupply of oil along with a disconnected strategic and political agenda has negatively affected the oil price and resulted in delayed and cancelled projects. This in turn has impacted the value chain and caused many companies and thousands of professionals to cease working in the oilfield at least for the moment.

As a former marine and current performance coach, I recognise and respect the significant efforts made by oilfield professionals daily and globally. Rig teams often battle weather conditions, logistical challenges, technical problems, crew diversity, and local hostility in order to make things happen and to get the job done.

Five transferable leading-success factors applicable to the battlefield and to the oilfield are as follows:

1. one team, one mission
2. respected leadership
3. thirst for learning
4. applied best practice
5. unwavering commitment

With these factors as a genuine aspiration, the chance of successfully achieving goals and objectives is exponentially increased. Battling to victory against enemy forces, market forces, or the forces of nature takes considerable and coordinated effort. Tough times call for tough people and tough decisions, but they also call for tailored solutions to troubleshoot specific obstacles.

With some battlefield and some oilfield experience, like many others, I see some similarity and an opportunity to benefit performance through shared reality. The conversation continues.

CHAPTER 41

WHAT DO WE MEAN BY CONGRUENCE?

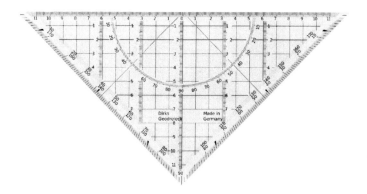

When triangles are congruent, one triangle can be moved (through one, or more, rigid motions) to coincide with the other triangle.

Personal congruence refers to a state in which a person's values and beliefs are consistent with the way that person lives his or her life.

For me the application of this principle is fundamental to credibility. If we were never to compromise the following rule, we would be well on our way to exceptional leadership and world-class performance.

> Rule: Do what we say we will do – when
> we say we will do it – every time.

Actions speak louder than words; actions need to coincide with our words which, indeed, themselves need to coincide with our genuine values and beliefs in order for true harmony, real authenticity, and effortless momentum to build.

Congruence is possibly the greatest secret to success. The alignment of what we value and believe with what we say and do is surely a powerful force. That said, turning the theory into actuality is difficult, perhaps a never-ending work in progress.

If we do manage to line it all up, we are likely to be highly valuable and extremely effective! Aim for congruence and increase your success rate.

CHAPTER 42

WHAT IS COGNITIVE DISSONANCE?

Progressing from low performance to high performance requires honest and frank conversations which confront reality and acknowledge failure. The mindset and toolkit to enable this culture ensures that continuous improvement can thrive and true learning can take place. Sounds straightforward but never is.

One of the phenomena that can derail an improvement campaign is something called "cognitive dissonance". In simple terms, this is the discomfort experienced by an individual who holds two or more contradictory beliefs, ideas, or values at the same time; performs an action that is contradictory to their beliefs, ideas, or values; or is confronted by new information that conflicts with existing beliefs, ideas, or values.

If we zoom in on the final point and consider it in the context of a learning campaign where this notional individual is a key leader, it can be a real blocker to progress, but even worse, it can be dangerous.

I am currently listening to the audio book *Black Box Thinking* by Matthew Syed. He provides some seriously concerning examples of cognitive dissonance. One involves a senior surgeon who refuses to change his latex gloves for other gloves despite a junior anaesthetist advising him that the patient is experiencing a latex allergy (and could die). The other reminds us of the issue of weapons of mass destruction (WMD) in Iraq and the fact that Western politicians for a long time refused to accept that there were none. In both cases, the embedded, existing beliefs of key leaders made it almost impossible for them to accept new evidence because they conflicted too starkly with everything these people believed, or had experienced, heard, or seen before.

As a performance coach, I have facilitated some challenging conversations during which key project leaders have struggled to accept "lessons learned", new ideas, practices, or even data because they have always done or perceived things a certain way. It reminds me of the old phrase "because we've always done it like that"!

We tend to look for evidence which supports our own beliefs. It is sometimes hard to accept that what we have believed for so long is, in fact, inefficient or even obsolete.

I used to believe that fitness training on my own was most cost-effective and efficient because I wasn't paying anyone and I knew what I wanted to improve. The concept of a personal trainer or class instructor used to be dissonant for me, as I felt

I had the qualification and motivation to train on my own, yet I was reading and hearing more and more about the benefits of external expert support. Eventually I altered my perception and for the last ten years have acted accordingly and seen significant personal fitness benefit through personal training and now CrossFit class workouts.

Cognitive dissonance can be a block to improvement, one to be aware of!

CHAPTER 43

WHO HAS THE MOST INSTINCTIVE TEAMWORK?

Instinct is an innate, typically fixed pattern of behaviour in animals in response to certain stimuli.

If we turn to the natural world, we can find some truly inspiring teamwork borne of survival instinct and experiential learning. If nothing else these well-researched behavioural patterns provide food for thought and promote wonderful admiration.

We'll consider three examples: one from the sea, one from land, and one from the air. We'll identify a striking idiosyncrasy for each and then pull it all together.

A pod of dolphins will circle and herd a school of fish into a tightly-packed "bait ball" and, if possible, even guide the fish into shallow water. Once there, the dolphins take turns ploughing through the bait ball, gorging on the fish as they pass through. Scientists have observed that dolphins have such control of this method that it is almost impossible for the fish to escape until each dolphin has had its fill. Working as a team, the dolphins are much more successful than if they'd worked alone.

A pack of wolves has a consistent order of march when moving from A to B; the three wolves at the front are the sick and elderly – they are sacrificial in the event of an ambush. Equally, their pace sets the tempo for the rest of the pack so that they do not get left behind. They are followed by the five toughest young wolves, then the rest of the pack, followed by another five tough wolves towards the rear. Trailing behind is the alpha wolf, surveying it all and maintaining strategic control. Each wolf does what is best for the pack. This approach applies to their every endeavour.

A flock of geese flies in a V formation so that each goose provides additional lift and reduced air resistance for the goose flying behind. By flying together in a V formation, scientists estimate that the whole flock can fly 70 per cent further with the same amount of energy than if each goose flew alone. The geese rotate positions to share the load, and they have learned that this team approach is the smart way to travel!

Many of us have come across these phenomena, and the transferable lessons are nothing new. However, a reminder and a picture, along with a description of the key facts, can restore our aspiration to emulate mother nature:

1. Individual success often relies on well-coordinated teamwork.
2. Extreme ownership of our team role ensures the team survives to succeed.
3. Smart organisation and collaborative effort helps the team go even further together.

I have always been instinctively inspired by excellent teamwork; feel free to share if you feel the same.

CHAPTER 44

AN ENCOURAGING REMINDER FOR HIGH PERFORMANCE

I have recently been fortunate enough to conduct a number of performance culture assessments on heavy-industry installations. This reminded me that I have now been involved in dozens of similar assessments in several sectors in the last twenty years, and there is one simple realisation which has been reinforced time and again through observation, perception, data analysis, and direct interviewee feedback.

The reinforced realisation is that, even with old equipment and average process, a group of people with exceptional servant-leadership and world-class teamwork, will challenge, and often outstrip, similar operations which boast newer equipment and more-advanced methodology.

Of course if you take an exceptional team and give it the best processes and most advanced technology, in theory the sky is the limit. In reality it is often the "underdog" label which inspires a benchmark team. Nonetheless, a well-led community of willing and proven volunteers with the right mindset and skillset is always preferable to a thousand pressed or egotistical men who lack motivation, drive, and cohesion.

There are indeed world-class organisations with the leadership, the team, leading technology and a trail-breaking approach – great examples from which we should try to learn.

Sadly, all too often I have encountered the flip side: new installations with the latest hardware and software, but a dysfunctional group of people. Without exception in these cases, there will be inconsistent and generally poor leadership. There will also be a collection of individuals, often very capable in their own right, who have not yet gelled as a cohesive unit and who are not yet striving to achieve a clear mission together.

My view is that it can be extremely difficult to help build a high-performing operation; there is no doubting that. But the first step, as with any transformational journey, is admission: admission that people are the most important component of any performance. Unless an investment is made in building a committed and well-led team, high performance will remain an elusive goal.

CHAPTER 45

WHAT CAN WE LEARN FROM RECENT ELECTIONS?

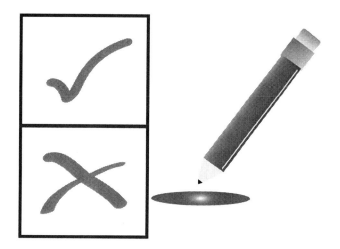

The year 2016 has had its share of surprises. These include "Brexit" and "Trumpet".

One significant observation after the UK and US elections was the outright refusal by many to accept the result of the democratic voting process. Further, it appeared that many key leaders had not truly kept in touch with reality.

Understandably, many people were frustrated and genuinely concerned about the future when the results were announced. But I want to focus on the disbelief and disdain; the leaders who refused to accept that their campaign assumptions could be incorrect.

Their "feedback denial" reminded me that in general we tend to have a reluctance to believe or accept feedback if it does not align with our perception of reality.

I have seen this phenomenon play itself out on project operations, and it can negatively affect safety, welfare, efficiency, and profit. It is often explained as a form of cognitive bias or a tendency to think in a way that deviates from rationality and good judgment.

For example, when performance is worse than expected on a deliverable, we as leaders can make assumptions about why the performance was suboptimal. Worst case, we can become deaf to the feedback from those involved, feedback which probably includes a number of contributing factors we do not want to hear. It may even include the fact that we are part of the problem.

Once again, reinforcement that the following components are key to sustained improvement and high performance:

1. servant-leaders
2. committed team
3. proven process
4. frank communication

Servant-leaders listen to the team and serve the team, not the other way around. A committed team takes extreme ownership and gets the job done.

A proven process includes listening to the views of the team and respecting the feedback. It includes planning and learning, analysing and recognising. It relies on frank communication which will only exist if the culture encourages that.

As with elections, project feedback is fundamental to project progress. Identified issues must be addressed, lessons must be learned, and the team must be heard. Leaders who ignore these points will one day lose the vote.

CHAPTER 46

HOW DO WE GET OUT OF OUR OWN WAY?

There is a Gary Larson *The Far Side* picture which has stayed with me since the first time I saw it; it involves a man pushing hard on a door that clearly says "Pull"! There is a simplicity about the individual, the picture, and indeed the message.

The applicable learnings for me are fourfold.

Be honest about my shortcomings! I have actually been the guy in that Larson picture pushing on a door which says pull. In fact, I think I have even had my hand on the word *pull* as I have been pushing before. I've also done the reverse and tried to pull on a door handle when the door says push :) I accept that I do not always read the instructions when I should, and as a result, I occasionally slow myself down or repeat previous mistakes. More than that, sadly my ego and need to be right can often cloud good judgment, common sense, and smart decisions for the greater good.

Consider the bigger picture. There is a well-known saying: "Can't see the wood for the trees". This refers to our tendency to become so immersed in the "doing" and detail of a task that we do not maintain a bigger-picture perspective on what else is going on in the world and, indeed, which other doors may be open to us.

Pause before the push: Too often I have rushed into a challenge without pausing to consider my rationale for investing the time and energy, the potential consequences of said investment, and the opportunity cost of taking on this particular challenge. A pause helps to clarify the strategy as well as the tactical approach. In this case, pulling the handle to take the first step forward might be a more successful start.

Apply experiential learning: It is essential to find a way to continue the improvement journey, to continue learning (from others and ourselves), to find our callings, and to escape the pattern of repeated mistakes. There is no one-size-fits all; each individual or team has unique DNA. To this end, generic best practice needs to be tailored to a specific solution for success. Whatever the personal recipe, "the proof will be in the pudding". Adapt accordingly.

Getting out of our own way is difficult, but it can be done. As a coach I have noticed that these steps can help leaders and teams to open the door to better performance; acknowledge the gaps, consider options, pause to rehearse the chosen plan, and keep learning in order to improve for next time.

Let me now see if I can get out of my own way.

CHAPTER 47

INSPIRED BY THE BLITZ BOKKE

The South Africa 7s team once again tops the IRB 7s world series standings after the first two tournaments in Dubai and Cape Town respectively. They are always combative and continue to play a brand of rugby which thrills fans and neutrals alike.

The word *blitz* means an intense sudden attack, an onslaught or bombardment, and it perfectly describes the way the Blitz Bokke play each game. Physically they have smaller players than squads like Fiji, but in every other way, they are larger than life. There is an extraordinary energy and ferocity to their approach, extreme commitment to the cause, and passion and panache to boot.

Contrast this with the current performance of the Springbok team. It is hard to believe they play different versions of the same sport for the same country!

If we consider the lagging indicators of high performance within the Blitz Bokke setup, we easily note the following: consistently top three in the world and winners of the Commonwealth Games in Glasgow 2014, phenomenal skill level, world-class commitment, behaviour of a close-knit family, visible elation when competing; and performing at the highest level.

If we then consider the leading indicators to understand the culture which is contributing to these consistently exceptional results, we can draw from a 2016 blog post by Werner Kok (voted onto the World 7s dream team) on a former captain's website.

"It really was a dream come true. Being part of this team means you have a small family who always has your back. They always support you and always push you to reach your goals. Believe me when I say, I have one of the best jobs in the world!

"Working hard and giving it our all at practice really paid off on game day. It's a case of input equals output. We were strong and consistent until the end. The best moment of this tournament was making the dream team with my captain, Kyle Brown. If you ask any one of the players, they would tell you how much it meant to me. It's the best feeling to see my name with some of the best players in the world. I'm going to continue to train hard, play hard, and help my team to victory, and try and make that dream team again."

Their style of play stems from a self-belief and camaraderie which is clearly evident. Most importantly, the Blitz Bokke inspire spectators around the world because they are achieving high performance whilst clearly enjoying themselves; they are as prepared as they need to be to perform on the world stage.

Thanks for the inspiration and a couple of useful reminders for a world-class team performance blitz: "input equals output" and drive a "dream team" champion mindset.

CHAPTER 48

WHAT IS THE BEST PERFORMANCE QUOTE?

I love inspiring quotes and have come up with a few of my own over the years. It got me thinking: Which are the best quotes when it comes to coaching high performance? Which quotes really pack a punch and make people want to roll up their sleeves and make a positive difference?

Of course, this is a subjective question, and different quotes will ignite different people for different reasons, but there are some quotes which have stood the test of time. Upon reflection, it did not surprise me to realise that these quotes are typically popular for three reasons: (1) authentic and genuinely appealing message which feels intuitively true even if hard to achieve/believe sometimes; (2) credible author who has proven his or her value to the world – "walked the talk"; and (3) the time that the quote was quoted – a general period or specific event which makes the message that much more poignant.

Michael Jordan's quote on the relationship between failure and success picks me up every time I am down: "I've missed more than nine thousand shots in my career. I've lost almost three hundred games. Twenty-six times, I've been trusted to take the game winning shot and missed. I've failed over and over and over again in my life. And that is why I succeed."

Albert Einstein is famed for many quotes; this one reminds me to avoid the comfort zone: "Anyone who has never made a mistake has never tried anything new."

Nelson Mandela is an icon for servant-leadership. This is one of many quotes from him which sums up the great man and reminds me to check my ego at the door and to lead the right way when I get a chance: "It is better to lead from behind and to put others in front, especially when you celebrate team success. You take the front line when there is danger. Then people will appreciate your leadership."

Martin Luther King brought together a divided nation through his courage, conviction, and faith. His quotes are famous. I chose this one as it resonates enormously for me: "We must develop and maintain the capacity to forgive. He who is devoid of the power to forgive is devoid of the power to love. There is some good in the worst of us and some evil in the best of us. When we discover this, we are less prone to hate our enemies."

Winston Churchill was a wartime leader who stood at the abyss and galvanised the Allies in history's darkest hour. His quote including the famous words "we will never surrender" is legendary, but his simpler version is just as powerful and applies on a daily basis: "Never, never, never give up."

Bringing it together for project performance, drawing on the right quote at the right time can be a game changer. There are also some quotes that have stood the test of time and are certainly valuable for performance improvement. Their messages make sense: Learning from failure leads to success, the learning takes place outside the known comfort zone, appropriate leadership is critical, forgiveness breaks down barriers, and most importantly, never, ever give up – you are closer than you think to achieving the dream!

CHAPTER 49

WHAT DOES IT MEAN TO FINISH STRONG?

Finishing strong can be harder than it sounds. Our natural human tendency is often to compromise our level of excellence as time passes by. Standards can slip as we experience "performance creep" whereby best practice is eroded and poor practice becomes acceptable.

In sport there are many examples of late comebacks and corresponding flops. "Snatching defeat from the jaws of victory" is a reference that no sports person or team wants to wear. Rather, "snatching victory from the jaws of defeat" would be more aligned with finishing strong.

An example of a strong performance but particularly a strong finish which sticks in my mind from the Rio Olympics is the world-record-breaking 400 metre win by South Africa's Wayde van Niekerk. He was running in the outside lane and therefore had no visibility of the other finalists. He was always in the lead, but he needed a strong finish if he was going to eclipse the 43.18-second world record set by the legendary Michael Johnson in 1999. As he came around the final bend and into the home straight, it initially seemed that he was being caught by the two pre-race favourites. However, van Niekerk was merely shifting gear. In the final 50 metres, he accelerated away from the field and destroyed the world record to set a new mark of 43:03. His strong finish was pure inspiration. He was named track athlete of the Rio Games.

Mo Farah is a GB favourite who also deserves mention for his incredible final laps to win the 5,000 metres at both the London and Rio Games! Having won the 10,000 metres at both games as well, he is now one of very few Olympians to have won the "double-double".

There are hundreds of examples from dozens of sporting codes, of strong finishes which ignite the crowd and rewrite the history books. But finishing strong is a differentiator far beyond the world of sport.

Research has shown that on heavy-industry projects and military campaigns there is generally an increase in accidents and incidents towards the end. This is put down to human factors such as a loss of focus, loss of leadership, and a compromised team approach as distractions and sometimes disillusionment or despondency creep in.

For this reason, it is vital that as a campaign winds down and the team is dissolved, a "best practice as usual"-performance-planning-and-learning approach is led through to the very end. Not only that, but ideally a project retrospect should be held with all key stakeholders after project demobilisation to ensure that lessons are captured, discussed, and ultimately applied to future project management and for future benefit.

At a macro level as with the micro level, too often the emphasis is placed on a winning start rather than a winning finish. Proper pacing is essential to guarantee consistency throughout performance. We talk about safety, efficiency, and consistency; perhaps we should add legacy as a strong reminder that a campaign is not successfully complete until the final operation is safely done, the troops are home, and the project retrospect is facilitated, filed, and closed.

Each calendar year is a campaign in its own right. For the last year, now a chance to finish strong and reflect on the legacy. For the next year, a chance to start well and apply lessons learned!

CHAPTER 50

WHAT IS THE BEST ADVICE YOU HAVE EVER RECEIVED?

I recently finished an interesting book by Richard Reed called "*If I Could Tell You Just One Thing …*". It is effectively a transcript of the interviews that Reed conducted with dozens of famous people, and the focus is on each celebrity's best piece of advice to those seeking success in life.

Of course, the first point is that we need to be clear on our own definitions of success; that has a fundamental bearing on which advice will make most sense. Secondly, we probably have to accept that, even with the same definition, advice that works for one may not work for another. That said, there were some interesting themes and it got me thinking about what advice I might give my children.

My gut-feel top-five are as follows:

1. Be yourself. Don't try to be someone else.
2. Do stuff you enjoy most of the time; this implies that you need to find work that you enjoy too!
3. Don't beat yourself up if you make a mistake; learn what you need to and move forward. Also, forgive others who make mistakes; you know how it feels to mess up so empathise and forgive, then provide support as necessary.
4. Show up – be present and prepared; "anything worth doing is worth doing well".
5. Never give up – success could be just around the corner.

One way or another, this list is some of the best advice I have received and, therefore, the advice I would be happiest to impart.

CHAPTER 51

WHAT DO WE MEAN BY THE BLAME GAME?

In my experience, nothing undermines and divides a team quite like blame. Blame generally involves declaring that someone or something (else) is responsible for a fault or wrong. Blame is also known as "finger pointing".

The opposite of blame is praise, recognition, and commendation.

Think for a moment about the difference in community morale between a culture where the predominant approach is blame versus one where praise is practiced most often. Which culture is more appealing to you? If the former, perhaps it's time for some personal reflection.

Interestingly one of the simplest catalysts for performance transformation at the project front line is that switch in emphasis from blame to recognition, from looking for what went wrong to looking for what went right.

The point is not that fault should be ignored; rather it is that team members should take ownership for our own roles, our own contributions, our own weaknesses, and when they happen, our own mistakes. In high-performance teams, this means that there is no need for blame because team members declare and own their mistakes before anyone else needs to say anything. Jocko Willink and Leif Babin talk about this in their book *Extreme Ownership*, an account of the US Navy Seals who overcame innumerable odds against insurgents in war-torn Iraq.

The Seals talk about managing up and down the chain of command so that miscommunication is avoided: Rather than "blaming" others, their approach is always to say, "What did I do to cause an issue?" and "What do I need to do to prevent a repeat?" If everyone takes this approach, mistakes go down, morale goes up, and success is achieved.

All too often in the modern boardroom, we notice leaders blaming poor results on anything but themselves. Especially disappointing is that we often see blame being apportioned to people who are not in the room.

It is not surprising that the most respected and inspiring leaders actively prevent blame and encourage ownership. Blame is a cancer that, if left unchecked, can decimate a team.

Perhaps we should all start with the question "what have I done to make a positive difference to the situation?" What a refreshing alternative that would be to the blame game.

CHAPTER 52

HOW SHOULD WE SET GOALS FOR NEXT YEAR?

I have always believed in setting targets and goals; as Zig Ziglar said, "If you aim at nothing, you will hit it every time." Setting goals for the next calendar year makes sense as there is a logical time measure.

Time is one of the key components of SMART goal setting, the much vaunted acronym for setting goals. There are a few variations but the one that I have found to be a good prompt is as follows:

Specific – be as clear and unambiguous as possible about what it is that you aim to achieve.

Measurable – ensure that there is a logical and satisfactory way by which you can measure whether or not the goal has been successfully achieved.

Adjustable – whether we like it or not, circumstances outside our control can sometimes affect the necessary conditions for the achievement of our original goals. When this occurs, it might be appropriate to adjust in order to maintain a goal.

Realistic – ensure the goal is at least feasible even if extremely challenging.

Time referenced – as mentioned initially, goals need a target completion date to provide some positive pressure and to promote a schedule based on the available time between now and the future target.

The Best Year Yet (BYY) process provides a good framework for reflecting on personal values, lessons learned, guidelines and goals. The well-developed concept helps people to focus on specific areas of their lives and to list the goals associated with those. Overall then, the top-ten goals can be finalised and pursued (including milestones along the way) through the ensuing year.

Another tool I have found to be very powerful is a vision board. This concept is discussed by some of the interviewees on the movie *The Secret* which went viral in the self-help community a decade ago; the interviewed high-achievers emphasise the proven value of creating and designing our desired future vision on a board in order to plant a subliminal homing beacon which will only be satisfied when the "visualised becomes actualised"!

In summary, goal setting can be optimised and cemented with SMART prompts, a solid framework such as BYY, and a corresponding vision board. Going this far will significantly enhance our chances of making a breakthrough next year. The hard truth, however, is that taking and tracking action is the vital next crucial step to actually achieving or perhaps even exceeding the goals we set.

Lightning Source UK Ltd.
Milton Keynes UK
UKOW03f0055050517
300542UK00001B/7/P